Conditionals
with
DISNEY·PIXAR
INCREDIBLES 2

Allyssa Loya

Ler

Lerner Publications Company
A division of Lerner Publishing Group, Inc.
241 First Avenue North
Minneapolis, MN 55401 USA

For reading levels and more information, look up this title at www.lernerbooks.com.

Additional graphics provided by Laura Westlund/Independent Picture Service.

Main body text set in Billy Infant Regular 14/20.
Typeface provided by SparkyType.

Library of Congress Cataloging-in-Publication Data

Names: Loya, Allyssa, author.
Title: Conditionals with The Incredibles 2 / Allyssa Loya.
Description: Minneapolis, MN : Lerner Publishing Group, Inc., [2019] | Series: Disney
    coding adventures | Includes bibliographical references and index. | Audience: Ages
    6-9. | Audience: Grades K to 3.
Identifiers: LCCN 2018002332 (print) | LCCN 2018021470
    (ebook) | ISBN 9781541524354 (eb pdf) | ISBN 9781541524309 (lb : alk. paper) |
    ISBN 9781541526785 (pb : alk. paper)
Subjects: LCSH: Conditional expectations (Mathematics)—Juvenile literature. |
    Conditionals (Logic)—Juvenile literature. | Incredibles 2 (Motion picture)—Juvenile
    literature.
Classification: LCC QA76.6115 (ebook) | LCC QA76.6115 .L69 2019 (print) | DDC
    511.3/17—dc23

LC record available at https://lccn.loc.gov/2018002332

Manufactured in the United States of America
1-44518-34768-4/18/2018

Table of Contents

What Are Conditionals?

Think about computer games you've seen. Game characters do so many things! They move left or right. They might jump, run, or spin. When an enemy appears, they attack!

How do computers know what characters should do? People write lines of code for computers. The lines of code are instructions. Conditionals are a type of code. They help a computer make decisions based on different conditions.

Imagine a game character running down a trail. The character meets a wall. Conditional code tells the character to jump over the wall. Conditionals can be shown in flowcharts like the one on the next page. The flowchart's first step asks if the character has come to a wall. If the answer is yes, the computer follows the path on the left. It tells the character to jump over the wall. If the answer is no, the computer follows the other path. The character keeps running.

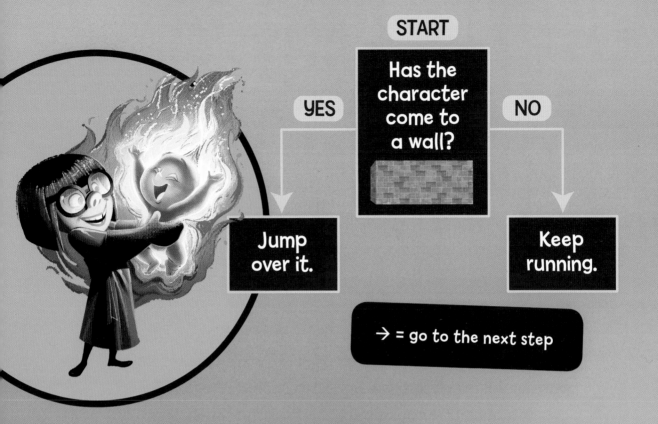

START

Has the character come to a wall?

YES

NO

Jump over it.

Keep running.

→ = go to the next step

You can help characters from *Incredibles 2* and learn about conditionals at the same time. You'll need a partner, plain paper, construction paper, a small stuffed animal, scissors, dice, and pencils for some of these activities.

Strike a Super Pose

The Incredibles strike super poses as they keep the city safe.

Find a partner. You'll pretend to be one of the Supers and strike poses. Face your partner from a few steps away. Your partner will count to three and then choose to either show you a thumbs-up or do nothing. Look at the conditional flowchart on the next page. Follow the flowchart's path on the right if your partner does nothing. That path leads to the action "Stand still." But if your partner gives you a thumbs-up, follow the left path. It's time to strike a pose!

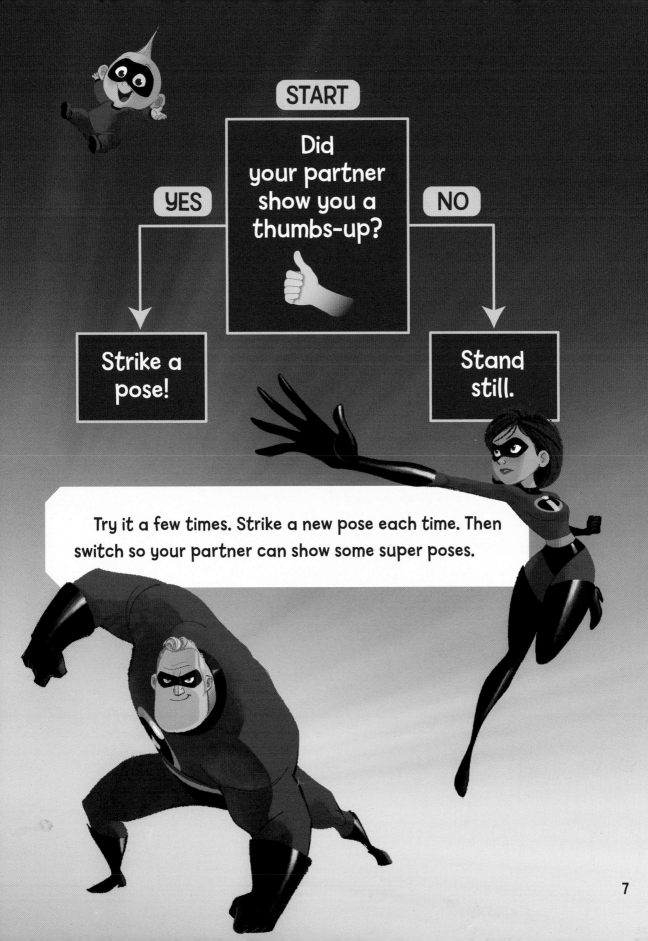

START

Did your partner show you a thumbs-up?

YES

NO

Strike a pose!

Stand still.

Try it a few times. Strike a new pose each time. Then switch so your partner can show some super poses.

7

Digging under the City

The Underminer is digging under the city to find bank vaults. He wants to steal the money inside them!

If the Underminer is not near a bank vault, he keeps digging. What will he do if he is near a vault? The conditional flowchart on the next page has a blank space. Look at the list of answer choices. On your own paper, write down the choice that the Underminer will take to steal the money from inside the vault.

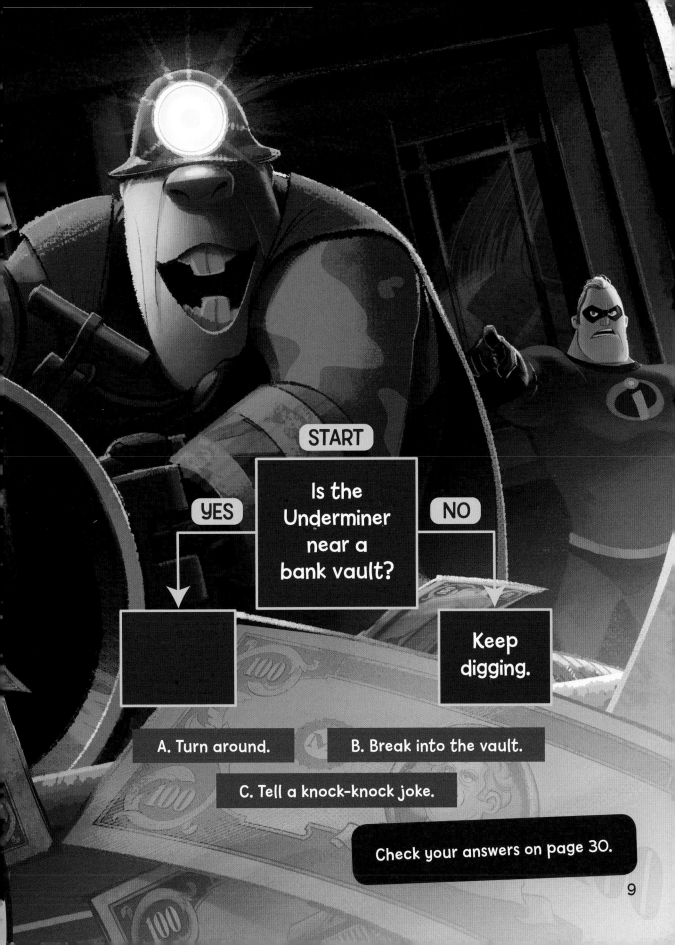

START

YES

Is the Underminer near a bank vault?

NO

Keep digging.

A. Turn around.

B. Break into the vault.

C. Tell a knock-knock joke.

Check your answers on page 30.

An Awesome New House

The Incredibles moved into a new house.
Help Dash explore their home.

Dash keeps bumping into things in the living room. He can run straight if no furniture is in his path. But he needs to turn if furniture blocks the way. Draw a flowchart on your own paper. It should look like the flowchart on page 11. Next, look at the list of actions. Choose one action to fill in each blank square. The flowchart should help Dash move around without bumping into furniture.

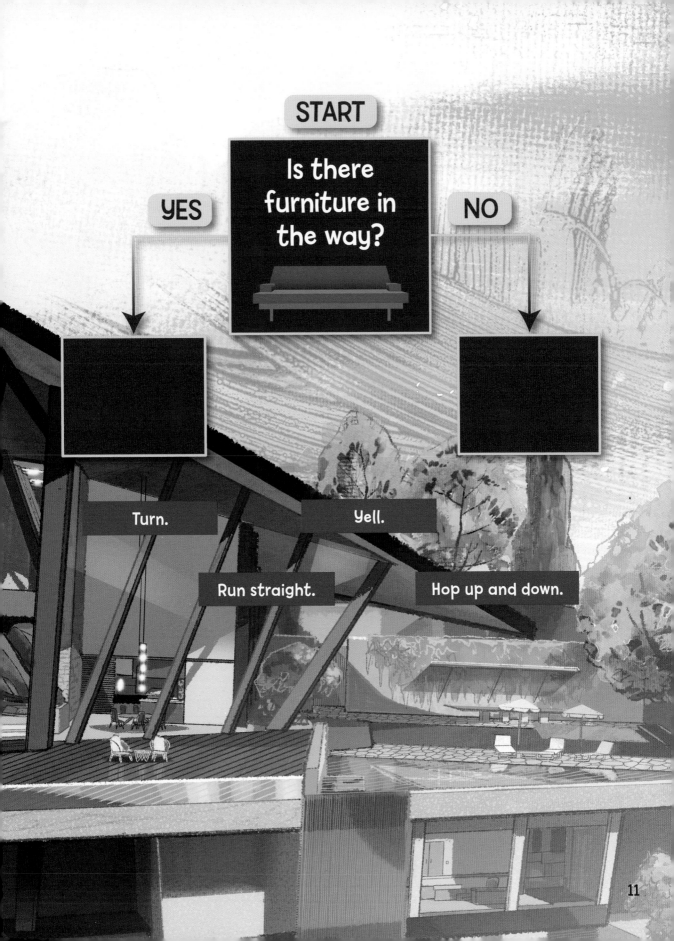

START

Is there furniture in the way?

YES

NO

Turn.

Yell.

Run straight.

Hop up and down.

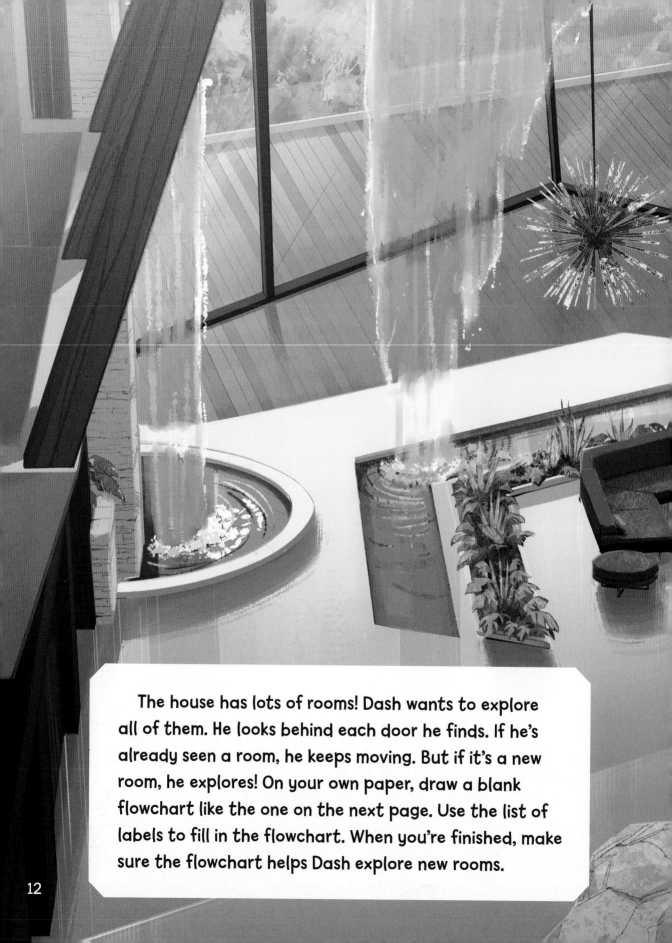

The house has lots of rooms! Dash wants to explore all of them. He looks behind each door he finds. If he's already seen a room, he keeps moving. But if it's a new room, he explores! On your own paper, draw a blank flowchart like the one on the next page. Use the list of labels to fill in the flowchart. When you're finished, make sure the flowchart helps Dash explore new rooms.

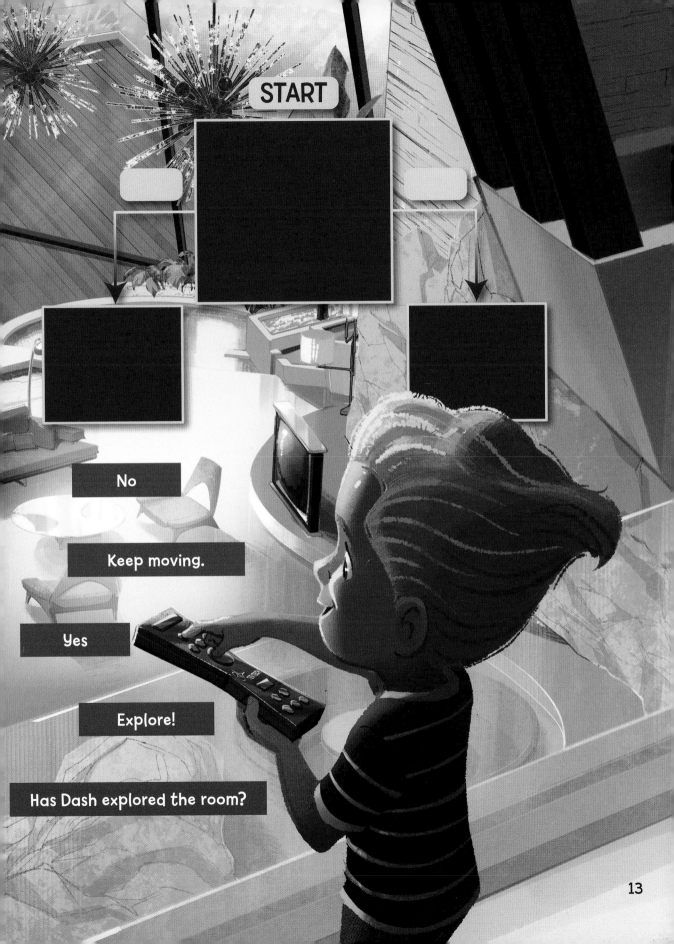

START

No

Keep moving.

Yes

Explore!

Has Dash explored the room?

13

Elastigirl on a Mission, Part 1

The MetroLev train is out of control! Elastigirl chases it across the city's rooftops on her Elasticycle.

Some lines of code have bugs, or errors. That means the code won't work properly. Each time Elastigirl comes to a gap between buildings, she must jump to the next roof. Look at the three flowcharts on page 15. Two of the flowcharts have bugs. Choose the flowchart with no bugs that will help Elastigirl catch the MetroLev.

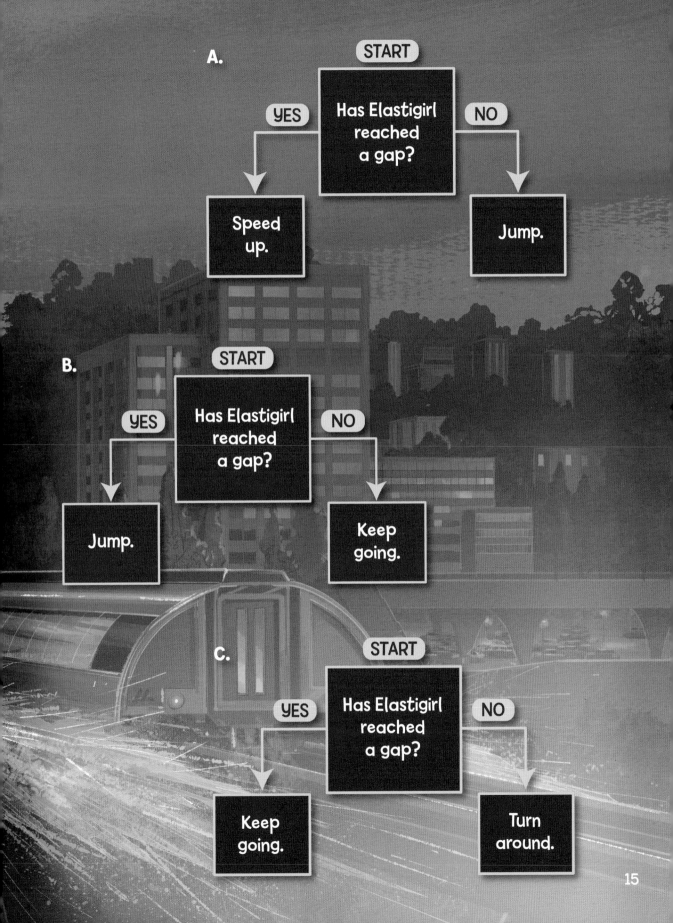

A.

START

Has Elastigirl reached a gap?

YES

NO

Speed up.

Jump.

B.

START

Has Elastigirl reached a gap?

YES

NO

Jump.

Keep going.

C.

START

Has Elastigirl reached a gap?

YES

NO

Keep going.

Turn around.

15

Bob's in Charge

Bob is watching the kids on his own. It's Jack-Jack's bedtime. Everything's going fine until Jack-Jack shoots laser beams from his eyes!

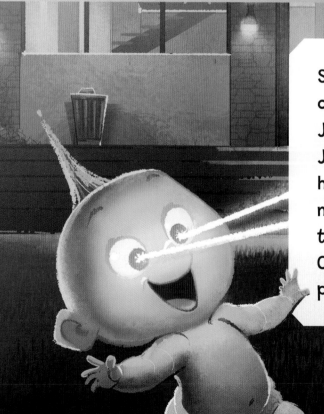

Sometimes code has more than one condition. Bob needs to catch Jack-Jack before he can put him to bed. Jack-Jack also needs to stop using his powers. The flowchart on the next page has a blank space where the second condition should go. Choose the answer that will let Bob put Jack-Jack to bed.

A. Did Jack-Jack finish his dinner?

B. Is Jack-Jack in bed?

C. Is Jack-Jack using his powers?

START

Did Bob catch Jack-Jack?

YES

YES

NO

Calm him.

Put him to bed.

Elastigirl on a Mission, Part 2

The Screenslaver is attacking a helicopter! Elastigirl needs to rescue the woman on board. But first, she has to find her.

Get a partner and a small stuffed animal. Pretend the stuffed animal is the woman in danger. You are Elastigirl. Close your eyes, and ask your partner to hide the woman somewhere in the room. Don't peek! When your partner is finished, open your eyes. Follow the flowchart on page 19 to find the woman. You can save her by picking her up. When you're finished, switch and have your partner search.

START

Search for the woman until you find her.

YES ← Is she safe? → NO

Strike a super pose.

Save her.

19

Supers Attack!

Supers under Screenslaver's control attack Jack-Jack, Dash, and Violet at home. They need to find a way to escape, fast!

When you brush your teeth, you move the brush in circles. You repeat the same step until your teeth are clean. Sometimes code must repeat steps too. Code with a loop repeats until a condition is met.

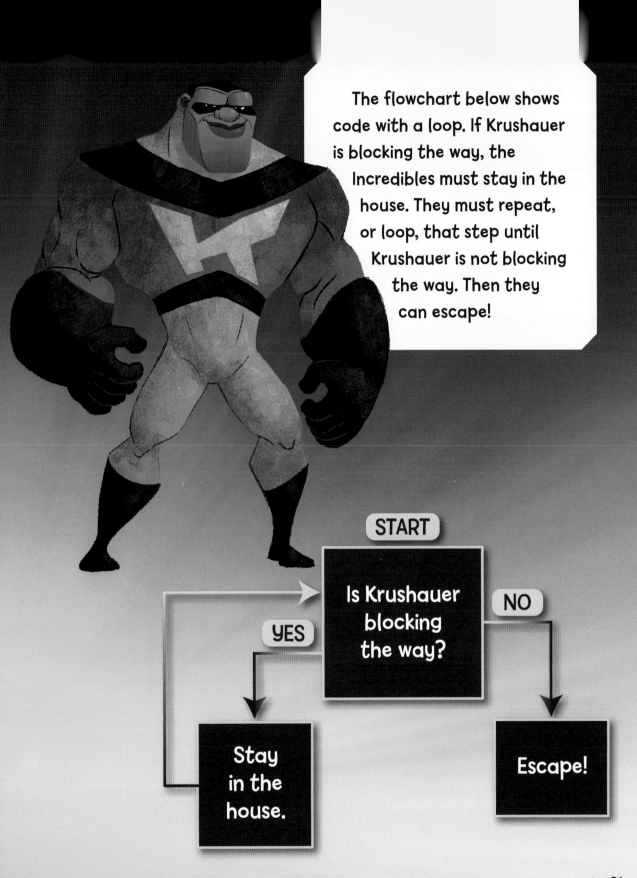

The flowchart below shows code with a loop. If Krushauer is blocking the way, the Incredibles must stay in the house. They must repeat, or loop, that step until Krushauer is not blocking the way. Then they can escape!

START

Is Krushauer blocking the way?

YES

NO

Stay in the house.

Escape!

21

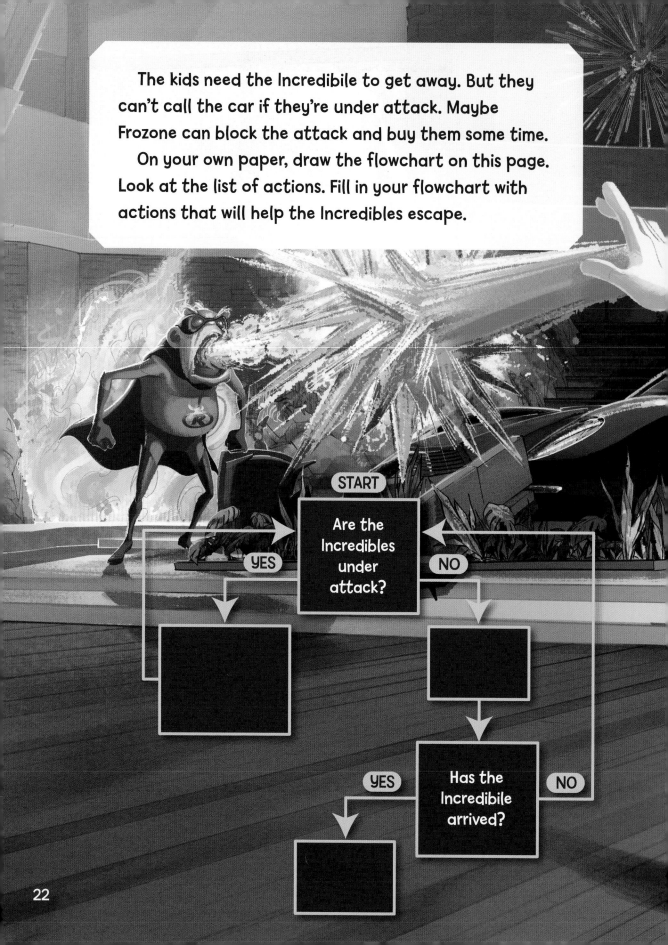

The kids need the Incredibile to get away. But they can't call the car if they're under attack. Maybe Frozone can block the attack and buy them some time.

On your own paper, draw the flowchart on this page. Look at the list of actions. Fill in your flowchart with actions that will help the Incredibles escape.

START

Are the Incredibles under attack?

YES

NO

YES

Has the Incredibile arrived?

NO

Drive away!

Frozone blocks the attack!

Call the Incredibile.

23

Mr. Incredible and Elastigirl Need Help

Violet, Dash, and Jack-Jack are racing to the DevTech boat in the Incredibile. Their parents are in trouble!

The Incredibile is an amazing machine. It can zoom down the road as a superfast car. On the water, it can turn into a boat! Look at the flowchart on the next page, and find the bugs, or places where the code won't work. Remember that when the Incredibile is on land, it needs to be a car. It should be a boat on the water. How would you rewrite the flowchart to fix the bugs?

START

Is the Incredibile on land?

YES

NO

Is it a car?

NO

YES

Is it a boat?

NO

Keep driving.

Change into a car.

Change into a boat.

Keep sailing.

Battle!

The kids found their parents on the DevTech boat. They need to fight together to defeat Supers under the Screenslaver's power.

Grab a pair of dice and at least one person to play this game with you. Decide who will be the Incredibles and who will be other Supers. Then look at the conditional flowchart on the next page for the rules. To start, each player rolls one of the dice. Follow the conditions and loops in the flowchart to play the game. Who will get ten points first? The winner of the game wins the battle!

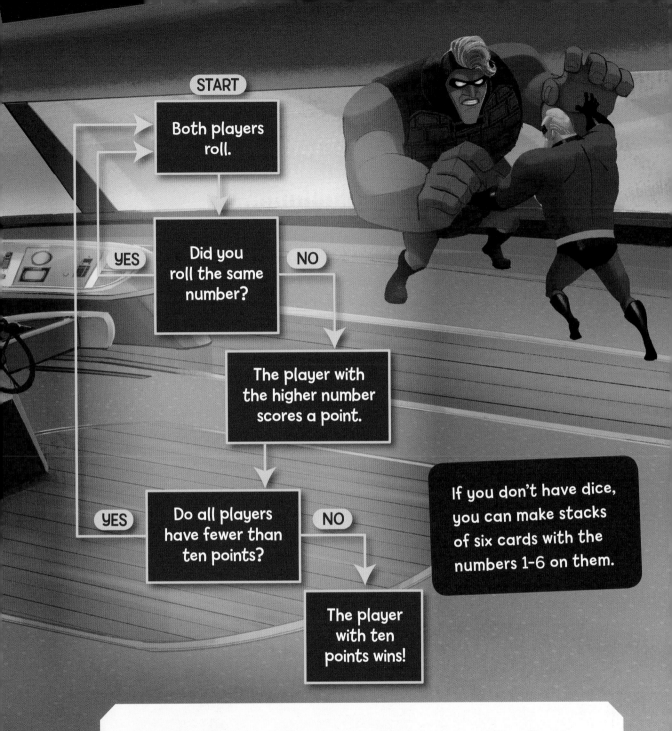

START

Both players roll.

YES — Did you roll the same number? — NO

The player with the higher number scores a point.

YES — Do all players have fewer than ten points? — NO

The player with ten points wins!

If you don't have dice, you can make stacks of six cards with the numbers 1-6 on them.

After you play a few times, make up your own rules. On your own paper, create a new flowchart that shows how the new rules work. One new rule might be that only odd numbers count. Another might be that the lowest roll wins. Or maybe rolling a certain number makes you win instantly!

You've learned so much about conditionals that you might start seeing them everywhere. If you think about it, lots of times conditionals help you make decisions. Do you have something to say at school? If the answer is yes, you might raise your hand. Is it raining during recess? Then maybe you will play in the gym instead.

Think about conditionals when you're at home too. Is your room clean? If so, you can go outside and play. But if it isn't, you might have to stay in and clean your room. Do you need help with your homework? If you do, ask someone. If not, take care of it yourself. You might be surprised by how often conditionals come up in your life!

Answer Key

Page 9: B

Page 11:

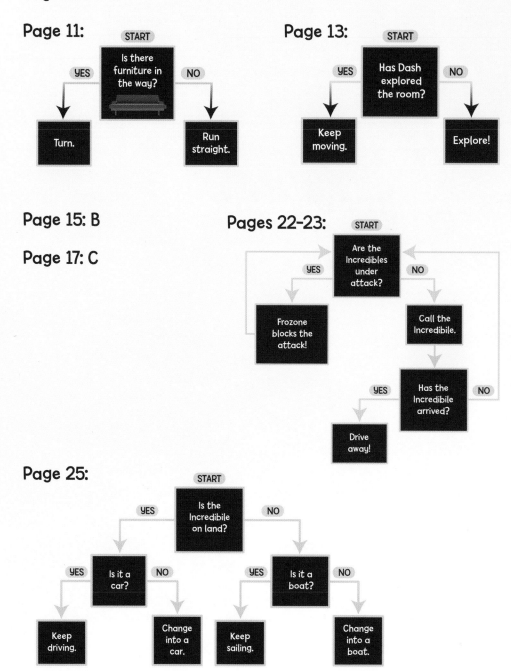

START
Is there furniture in the way?

YES → Turn.

NO → Run straight.

Page 13:

START
Has Dash explored the room?

YES → Keep moving.

NO → Explore!

Page 15: B

Page 17: C

Pages 22-23:

START
Are the Incredibles under attack?

YES → Frozone blocks the attack!

NO → Call the Incredible.

Has the Incredibile arrived?

YES → Drive away!

NO →

Page 25:

START
Is the Incredibile on land?

YES → Is it a car?

YES → Keep driving.

NO → Change into a car.

NO → Is it a boat?

YES → Keep sailing.

NO → Change into a boat.

Glossary

bug: a mistake found in lines of code

code: instructions for computers that are written in a way that computers can follow

condition: something that must happen before something else happens

loop: code that tells a computer to repeat an instruction a certain number of times

Further Information

CodeMonkey
https://www.playcodemonkey.com

Code.org
https://code.org/learn

Kelly, James F. *The Story of Coding*. New York: DK, 2017.

Lyons, Heather, and Elizabeth Tweedale. *Coding, Bugs, and Fixes*. Minneapolis: Lerner Publications, 2017.

Prottsman, Kiki. *My First Coding Book*. New York: DK, 2017.

Index

About the Author

Allyssa Loya is an elementary school librarian in North Texas. Her passion for bringing meaningful learning to students led her to cultivate a technology-forward library that includes a makerspace and a coding club. While running the coding club in the library, she realized how important it is for every student to experience coding. Not every student will grow up to be a computer programmer, but all students will need to know how to think clearly and critically when they are adults.

Loya is married to an IT manager, who is a perfect support system for her technological endeavors. Her two young boys are a constant reminder of the experiences that all students deserve from their educators.